Walt Disney's
Mickey
and His Friends

S0-DOQ-785

GOLDEN PRESS • NEW YORK

Western Publishing Company, Inc.
Racine, Wisconsin

Contents

Donald Duck, Animal Lover

"Unca Donald, look!" cried Dewey Duck. "Look what we found!"

"We found a baby raccoon on our hike!" said Huey Duck.

"He's all alone, Unca Donald," added Louie. "Something must have happened to his mama."

Donald Duck had been taking a nap under a tree in the heart of the big woods. Now he opened his eyes and looked at the little raccoon Huey was carrying. It looked back at him like a small, frightened bandit.

"We'd better take him to the animal shelter," said Louie. "He's too young to stay alone."

"Why can't *we* keep him?" said Donald.

"What?" cried the boys.

"Last year," said Donald, "Gladstone Gander won the Animal Lover's Prize at the Pet Show because he took in a stray cat. The year before that, Gyro Gearloose got the prize for being nice to birds. This year I could win!"

"But raccoons aren't like cats," said Louie.

"Or like birds, either," warned Dewey.

"No, they're cuter," said Donald. He took the raccoon from Huey. "We'll name him Rufus. This is going to be fun!"

It was fun, for a while.

Donald and the boys drove home with the raccoon and they took turns feeding him milk out of a small nursing bottle.

The days passed. Rufus ate and ate. He grew and grew. Soon he wasn't a baby raccoon anymore. He was a young raccoon who liked to romp around.

He was romping in the dining room one day while Donald and the boys were eating lunch. Rufus jumped up on the table and grabbed some food and ran.

"You thief!" yelled Donald. "Stop that!"

"He can't help it," said Louie. "He's getting too old for milk."

"Raccoons like fish," said Dewey.

"We read that in the Junior Wood-chuck Guide," declared Huey.

Donald grumbled and muttered, and he and the boys went off to the market and bought cans and cans of tuna fish for Rufus. But when they got home, Rufus wasn't anywhere to be seen.

"Rufus?" called Donald. "Where are you?"

"Listen!" said Huey.

From upstairs came the sound of water running.

Donald and the boys raced up to the bathroom. And there they saw that Rufus, with his clever little paws, had turned on the faucets. The raccoon was under the shower, and he was very wet. The bathroom was very wet. And Rufus was washing a piece of soap—and washing it and washing it.

"Rufus!" screamed Donald.

Rufus calmly ate the soap. Then he hiccupped a loud hiccup and ran out of the bathroom.

"I thought raccoons ate fish!" cried Donald.

"Raccoons eat everything," said Huey.

"And they like to wash things before they eat them," said Dewey.

"I read it in the Junior Woodchuck Guide," explained Louie.

Just then there was a horrible crash from downstairs.

Donald and the boys ran down. Rufus had gotten into the cupboard. He had tumbled all the pots out onto the floor. Now he was crouched on top of the refrigerator. He looked like a startled young bandit.

"You pick those up this instant!" shouted Donald.

"He can't," said Dewey.

"That's right," added Louie.

"It says so in the Junior Woodchuck Guide on page . . ."

"QUIET!" yelled Donald, interrupting Louie.

So the boys very quietly picked up the pots.

And Rufus very quietly curled up on top of the refrigerator and went to sleep.

More days passed, and Rufus grew and grew and grew some more. He became a large raccoon indeed.

He became a large raccoon who liked the shower so much that Donald had to keep the bathroom door locked.

He became a large raccoon who got into the flour canister and then left white footprints all over the house.

He became a large raccoon who got into the sugar bowl and washed all the sugar cubes until they melted and ran down the drain.

He became a large raccoon who liked to watch television with Donald and the boys. And he often drank Donald's soda pop while he watched.

"Raccoons like soda pop," said Louie one evening.

"Great!" snapped Donald. "Tell me

what raccoons don't like and I'll get lots of it."

"We told you," said Dewey. "Raccoons like everything."

Donald groaned. Then he remembered that the Pet Show was only a month away. And he went up to bed thinking about the prize he was going to win for being nice to Rufus.

In the middle of the night, Donald woke up. Someone was downstairs in the living room. Someone was talking in a deep voice.

"Burglars!" said Donald, and he called the police.

The police came quickly, but they didn't find any burglars. They found Rufus, sitting in front of the television set and peeling a banana with his clever little paws. He was watching the late-late-late show.

"I guess my raccoon figured out how to turn the television on," said Donald.

"Your raccoon, eh?" said one policeman, looking at Donald.

"Yes," said Donald.

7

The second policeman took out his ticket book. "You aren't allowed to keep wild animals in this neighborhood," said he. "You aren't allowed to keep lions or tigers or timber wolves or zebras or giraffes. Most especially, you aren't allowed to keep raccoons."

And the policeman gave Donald a ticket and went away.

"What am I going to do?" moaned Donald.

"Take Rufus back to the woods," said Huey.

"But then I won't win the prize," said Donald.

"Do you really care?" asked Dewey.

"No," said Donald. "I guess I really don't."

Bright and early the next morning, Donald and the boys went back to the woods with Rufus. They put the rac-coon down in a clearing where there was a nice stream.

Rufus went straight to the stream and found a pebble. He washed it. Then he found a crayfish and washed that—and ate it. He seemed to like it as well as he liked canned tuna fish.

Rufus climbed up a big tree and crept into a hollow place just above a stout branch. He peeped out of the hollow at Donald and the boys. He looked like a happy bandit indeed. He looked like a raccoon who was all ready to settle down in his own little den.

Donald and the boys left him and went home.

"You didn't really yell at Rufus too much," said Louie to Donald.

"So you *are* an animal lover," said Dewey.

"Even if you don't get a prize for it," said Huey.

Donald grinned. Because of him, there was a fat and happy raccoon living in the woods where he belonged. And that was prize enough.

The Solid Gold Paint Set

Daisy Duck and Clara Cluck were driving down Main Street, and when they passed the McDuck Money Bin, they saw Uncle Scrooge. The world's richest duck was standing beside his money bin. He was waving his arms and shouting.

"Those blasted kids! Look what they did to my beautiful money bin."

Daisy and Clara stopped. There on the wall of the money bin was a drawing done with spray paint. It was a drawing of a little duck with arms and legs made of sticks. The little stick duck had a top hat and eyeglasses and side-whiskers. It looked like Uncle Scrooge.

"World's Stingiest Miser!" was printed under the drawing.

"I'll show them!" shouted Uncle Scrooge. "I'll buy up every can of spray paint in town!"

And Uncle Scrooge stomped off to the hardware store on Main Street and bought every can of spray paint in the place. Then he carried all the sacks and cartons of spray paint to his money bin, where he hid them in the deepest, darkest vault he had.

Bright and early the next day, Daisy and Clara were again driving down Main Street. Again they came to the money bin, and again they saw Uncle Scrooge leaping and screaming and waving his arms.

"Another temper tantrum, and no

9

wonder," said Daisy. She pointed to the money bin. There was a second drawing of a stick figure. Underneath it someone had written, "The Meanest Millionaire In Town!"

Daisy and Clara rushed to comfort the angry old duck.

"There, there!" said Daisy to Uncle Scrooge. "I'm sure whoever did that drawing really didn't mean it."

"But where did the paint come from?" said Clara. "I thought you bought all the spray paint in town."

"That isn't spray paint!" screamed Scrooge. "That's house paint!"

Then he stopped his screaming and his fussing. "I bought all the spray paint and buried it in my money bin," he

THE MEANEST MILLIONAIRE IN TOWN!

said. "I can buy all the house paint, too."

Then he called his men to paint the money bin again, and he charged off and bought every can of house paint he could find. He bought green paint and blue paint and white paint and yellow paint. Then, to be on the safe side, he bought all the watercolors and all the poster paints for miles around. He had the paint delivered to his money bin, and he hid all of it away in the second deepest, darkest vault there.

The next morning Daisy and Clara found Uncle Scrooge outside his money bin. He wasn't leaping or screaming or waving his arms or shouting. He was just standing there like a poor, defeated old duck.

For someone had written, "Scrooge McDuck Is A Dope!" on the money bin. The writing was in colored chalk and it was ten feet high!

"You could buy up all the colored chalk in town," said Clara helpfully.

"It wouldn't do any good," Uncle Scrooge sobbed. "They'd think of something else—like felt-tipped pens. Besides, I have seventeen-thousand-cubic acres of paint in my money bin. If I buy more paint, there won't be room for my money."

"Then if you can't lick them, join them," said Daisy Duck, and she whispered something into Uncle Scrooge's ear. He perked right up.

"Why that's quite clever!" said Uncle Scrooge. "And I know what I could use for a prize. The Sultan of Bumpamore sent me a little gift last week—a gross of solid gold paint sets. I'll give one of them away."

"Perfect!" said Daisy.

"Let's get busy!" said Uncle Scrooge, and he bustled off to order his men to wash the chalk off the money-bin wall.

While he did this, Clara and Daisy hurried to the printer, where they had stacks and heaps of handbills made up. Then they walked down Main Street giving handbills to all the small people they met—and to the big ones as well.

They had signs made, too. They put these in shop windows. "Big Painting Contest Today!" read the signs. "Decorate the McDuck Money Bin! Win a Solid Gold Paint Set for the Most Beautiful Wall Painting!"

11

By the time Daisy and Clara got back to the money bin, crowds of little folk—and lots of big ones—were surging around the place. Huey, Dewey, and Louie were there, and so were all the other Junior Woodchucks. The Midtown Bowling League left the bowling alleys to enter the contest. The Society to Save the Elm Trees forgot about elms for the moment. Each and every member was eager to decorate Uncle Scrooge's money bin.

Of course there were many people who didn't belong to a league or a society. There were many people who only liked to paint on walls. Some had long ladders and some had short ladders and some hadn't bothered with ladders, but had just brought brushes.

Naturally Uncle Scrooge was there. The canny old millionaire had put up a stand on the steps of the money bin, and he was selling jars of poster paint. And, since Scrooge owned every smidgen of paint in town, everyone who wanted to enter the contest had to buy paint from him. He soon had quite a nice pile of cash, and everyone in town had paint.

"Is everyone ready?" said Uncle Scrooge at last. "Let's begin!"

And the great painting contest was underway!

You can be sure that no one who entered Uncle Scrooge's painting contest drew insulting little figures of Uncle Scrooge on the walls of the money bin. No one wrote that Uncle Scrooge was a miser or a mean old duck. Instead, peo-

ple drew pictures of flowers and trees and birds and bees and meadows and mountains and ships at sea.

Soon the walls of the money bin were covered, and there were paintings on the sidewalk and on the front steps and on the doors.

"All right!" called Scrooge. "Time's up! Put down your brushes."

Then he looked at all the pictures of the birds and bees and meadows and trees, and he decided that they were very nice—very nice indeed. But the nicest one of all, he thought, was the small painting that a very little Junior Woodchuck had painted on the mailbox. It showed a rather large ladybug sitting on a leaf, talking with a rather small caterpillar.

So the solid gold paint set was awarded to the little Woodchuck, and the crowd cheered. Then they all went off to their homes chatting happily to one another about what a fine time they had had decorating the money bin.

No sooner had they gone than there was a muttering and a grumbling and a growling sound from the sky.

"I do believe it's going to rain," said Clara Cluck, looking up at the big dark clouds over the money bin.

Rain it did. It rained torrents and torrents. The lightning flashed and the thunder crashed—and every bit of poster paint was washed off the walls of the money bin—and off the sidewalk and the steps and the front doors and even off the mailbox.

"Heavens to Betsy!" said Uncle Scrooge, when the storm had passed. "Look at my money bin! The walls are plain white again. By tomorrow somebody will have gotten some paint from somewhere and painted another one of those—ugh!—pictures of me!"

"Not if you give another contest," said Daisy Duck.

Uncle Scrooge looked upset. "I may have to hold a painting contest and give away a paint set every time it rains," he told Daisy and Clara.

"You do have a gross of the paint sets," Daisy said.

Uncle Scrooge brightened up. "That's true," he said. "And by the time they're gone . . ."

"By the time they're gone," said Daisy, "everybody will be tired of painting on walls."

Then Daisy pointed to a place in the street where the poster paints had mixed with the rainwater. "In the meantime," said Daisy, "it's fun to live in a place that has rainbows in the puddles to match the ones in the sky."

And Uncle Scrooge agreed that it was indeed.

The Misplaced Mermaid

All day long, Mickey Mouse and his nephews had fished in the mountain lake.

And what had they caught?

Well, Morty had landed an old tennis shoe.

Ferdie had hauled in a soggy straw hat.

Mickey himself had hooked a wading boot.

"I don't think there *are* any fish in this lake," said Ferdie, as the sun began to set.

"There's too much other stuff," said Morty.

"We might as well go home," said Mickey, and he began to row toward shore.

Suddenly Morty cried, "My gosh!"

Ferdie shouted, "Golly!"

Mickey stared. He rubbed his eyes and then stared some more.

A mermaid was sitting on a rock beside the lake, dangling her tail in the water.

"Please don't leave," said the mermaid. "Stay and talk with me. It's lonely here since all the fish went away."

Mickey and the boys didn't know what one said to a mermaid. It didn't matter. What the mermaid really wanted was someone to listen.

"My name is Melanie," said the mermaid. "I live in this lake. I always have. In the past, it was fun, but it isn't now. People come and throw things they

don't want into the water. That's why the fish went away."

A big tear rolled down the mermaid's cheek.

Mickey and the boys could see right away that no mermaid could be happy in a lake that was littered with boots and shoes and bits of trash. And they could see that any mermaid would be lonely when there weren't any fish to play with.

"Why not go to the ocean?" asked Mickey.

"There are lots of fish there," said Morty.

"Maybe there are other mermaids," said Ferdie hopefully. "I've heard that mermaids *do* live in the ocean."

Of course Ferdie had heard this. He hadn't really believed it until he met Melanie. He hadn't really believed that mermaids lived anywhere. But it might have seemed rude to say this, so Ferdie didn't say it. Instead, he told Melanie about coral reefs and sparkling waters—and schools and schools of fish.

"How far is it to the ocean?" asked Melanie. "My tail gets dry if I'm out of the water too long."

"It's not very far," said Mickey.

"And don't worry about your tail," said Morty. "It won't dry out."

Mickey and the boys had brought their lunch with them in a portable ice chest. They emptied the chest and filled it with water.

"You can sit in this," said Ferdie.

Melanie hopped into the ice chest, which turned out to be exactly the right size for a mermaid. Mickey and the boys lifted the chest into the back of Mickey's camper. Then they drove off into the sunset.

It was dark when they reached the ocean, but the moon was coming up. Melanie could sit in the ice chest at the

edge of the surf and look out across the waves.

"Isn't it keen?" said Morty.

"It's . . . it's very big," said Melanie.

"Sure it's big," said Ferdie. "It goes on forever. You can swim around the world from here."

"I don't think I want to swim *that* far," said Melanie. But she jumped into the water.

"Why, it's salty," said Melanie.

"Oceans are that way," said Morty.

"You'll get used to it," said Mickey.

But way out in the bay, some huge creature leaped out of the water, then came down again with a mighty splash.

"A monster!" cried Melanie. "Help! A monster is out there!"

"That's no monster," said Mickey. "It's probably a nice, friendly dolphin."

"I don't want to meet him!" I don't like the ocean. It's too salty. And too big. But my own nice lake is full of . . . full

of old shoes!" And Melanie began to weep and wail.

There was no help for it. Mickey and the boys had to take the little misplaced mermaid home. They put her in the bathtub so that her tail wouldn't dry out. "Maybe we could get some goldfish to keep her company," said Ferdie.

"I've got a better idea," said Mickey, and he went to the telephone and called all of his friends. He called Minnie Mouse and Goofy and Clarabelle Cow and Horace Horsecollar and Donald Duck. They all said that they'd love to help clean old boots and shoes out of a mountain lake so that the fish could swim there again.

Mickey didn't tell his friends about the mermaid. They might not have believed him. But early the next morning,

Mickey left Melanie snug and safe in the bathtub, and he and the boys set out for the lake. Horace and Minnie and the others went, too. They had cars and trucks and boats. They had rakes and hoes and grappling hooks.

They worked hard all day. They hauled the boots and shoes out of the lake. They also hauled out old tires and rusty bedsprings and sandwich wrappers and empty tin cans and bottles and jars.

When the lake was quite, quite clean, Horace Horsecollar piled the great heap of trash into his truck and drove off to the city dump.

Then Mickey and Donald Duck and Goofy dashed to the fish hatchery. There they got gallons and gallons of little fish. They got some big fish, too. They carried the fish to the lake and dumped them into the water.

The little fish scooted straight to the bottom, as if they were frightened. But the big fish jumped and splashed.

"The fishermen will be glad," said Minnie Mouse.

"I'm not worried about fishermen," said Mickey. And he and the boys hurried home.

Melanie had spent the day happily enough. She had washed her long hair twenty-seven times and had gotten suds all over the bathroom floor. But Mickey didn't mind. He and the boys put Melanie into the portable ice chest and took her to her own dear lake.

The little mermaid clapped her hands when she saw what Mickey and his friends had done. She jumped into the lake and swam and splashed. She chased the big fish. She dove to the bottom and tickled the little fish. She was as delighted as a mermaid can be.

Mickey and the boys were delighted, too. But they never fished in that lake again. They were afraid they would catch a trout or a minnow that might be a friend of Melanie's. And that would never do!

The Washout

"There!" said Bertram Beaver. He sat
on his tail, as beavers do, and looked
proudly at his new dam. It held back
the stream that once had run across the
meadow. It was a very solid dam, made
with logs and branches and sticks and
stones and mud.

"That keen," said Chip, in his chip-
munk fashion. "But why you build a
new dam?"

"Old one on creek still good," said
Dale.

"Oh, I like to work. Busy is the way
to be, if you're a beaver. And now that
my new dam is finished, I'll build a new
lodge."

Bertram peeped over the edge of his
dam. The water in the stream had
backed up nicely. Already there was
quite a deep pond behind the dam. Bertram dived into the pond and began to
swim about, looking for the right spot
to build a lodge.

Chip and Dale watched for a min-
ute. Then they started down to the
meadow. Suddenly Chip stood still and
pointed. "Lookie!"

There was a tent on the meadow
just below Bertram's dam.

"Campers," said Dale. "Let's go see. Maybe they have goodies for hungry chipmunks."

But when the two curious chipmunks reached the camp on the meadow, they forgot all about goodies. For the campers were no ordinary campers. Three dreadful Beagle Boys had come to the meadow.

"They bad guys!" said Chip.

"Shhh!" warned Dale. "They such bad guys, they step on us if they see us. Keep down."

The Beagles didn't see the chipmunks. The Beagles were busy laughing and boasting about how they had broken out of jail and swiped the tent and the camping gear from a sporting goods store.

"And nobody will ever come looking for us on this crummy mountain," said one of them. "We can hide out here forever."

With that, he began to build a fire. And with that fire, the trouble began. For the Beagles did not know the first thing about fires. Or perhaps they didn't care, which is just as bad.

They didn't dig a pit for the fire to keep it from spreading.

They didn't watch the fire.

And that night, when they went to sleep, they didn't put the fire out.

Chip and Dale and all of their friends were frightened. They took turns watching the camp to make sure the tall meadow grass didn't catch fire. Once, the fire did begin to spread, and Thumper the rabbit stamped it out with his big, thumping feet.

"This is awful," said Oliver Owl, the day after the Beagles made their camp. Oliver was perched in a tree near Bertram's dam. He was cross and sleepy. The smoke from the fire had blown into his own tree and awakened him.

"At least you pretty safe," said Chip.

"If dopey Beagles set the meadow on fire, you can fly away."

"And Bertram Beaver can hide in his pond," Dale pointed out.

"If the Beagles set the meadow on fire, it will be very crowded in my pond," declared Bertram. *"Everybody* will have to take shelter there."

This was certainly true. Chip and Dale wondered whether there would be room for everybody in the pond. But suddenly Chip had an idea.

"Bertram, you like to be busy beaver. How you like to unbuild a dam?"

"Unbuild a dam?" Bertram thought

about this. "It's an interesting idea," he said. "It might be fun for a change."

"Good," said Chip, and he told him about his plan.

"Excellent!" said Bertram. He set to work. He gnawed away a log from one part of his dam. He pulled some branches from another part. He took out some stones. He washed away some of the mud that was packed behind the branches.

Before long, Bertram didn't have a fine, stout dam. Bertram had a flimsy, wobbly dam—and a very large pond of water.

"I'll warn the animals to leave the meadow," said Oliver Owl, and he flew away to do it.

Soon every large and small creature who lived on the meadow had hurried to the high ground above Bertram Beaver's pond. Thumper was there with all of his brothers and sisters. The meadow mice had come scampering, and the badger had left his burrow and waddled to the high ground to join the opossums and the moles.

When everyone was ready, Chip and Dale each took an armload of acorns. They scooted down to the camp and began to pelt the Beagle Boys with acorns.

"Hey!" shouted one Beagle.

"Ouch!" cried the second Beagle.

"Cut that out!" yelled the third.

Chip and Dale chattered and jumped up and down and made faces at the Beagles.

Of course the Beagles began to chase the chipmunks. And of course Chip and Dale ran. They ran straight to Bertram Beaver's wobbly, flimsy dam. Then they ran across the top of the dam.

The Beagles pounded after them. And when the Beagles got to the middle of the dam, there was a mighty cracking and creaking and groaning from the dam. Then there was a mighty crunch, and the dam gave way.

"Help!" shouted one of the Beagles.

You can be sure that no one helped. The water from Bertram's fine pond swept through the broken dam. It roared down and across the meadow, carrying the Beagles with it. When it reached the camp, it picked up the tent and carried that along, too.

And of course it put out the fire.

The Beagles disappeared down the hill beyond the meadow. Oliver Owl flew after them. Before long he flew back to report. "Two rangers captured the Beagles at the foot of the mountain," said Oliver excitedly.

The animals cheered. They thanked Bertram for the use of his pond. They thanked Chip and Dale for being clever and brave.

Bertram was most pleased. And he set to work right away to rebuild his dam and make another pond. He knew that busy was the way to be. He also knew that a pond is a handy thing to have—especially if there are careless folk like the Beagles about.

Instant Garden

"Grow, blast you! Grow!" shouted Donald Duck.

Gyro Gearloose looked over the fence into Donald's yard. Donald was standing beside the front porch, glaring at a scrawny little rose bush.

"Look at that!" Donald pointed at the rose. "I planted it last week, and nothing's happened. Not a new leaf. Not a bud."

"Aren't you expecting a lot in a week?" asked Gyro.

"It'll be the same next week," Donald predicted. "And the week after that, and the week after that." Donald pointed to the drooping pansies beside the walk and the wretched petunias near the fence. "Nothing grows for me," he complained.

"Do you water them and feed them?" said Gyro.

"You sound just like Daisy!" cried Donald angrily. "She says that all the time." Donald scowled. "Daisy's garden is terrific."

Gyro laughed. "What you want is no work and an instant garden. Well, maybe I can help. I've just invented a formula for something I'm going to call Speedy-Gro. I'm not sure about it. I haven't tested it yet, but if it works the way I hope it will . . ."

"It'll make things grow?" asked Donald.

"I think so," said Gyro.

"What are we waiting for?" cried Donald. "Let's get some and sprinkle it around."

"You spray it with a spray gun," said Gyro.

"Okay, okay. We'll spray it!" said Donald.

He and Gyro ran off to Gyro's workshop, where Gyro gave Donald a rather large spray gun and a warning. "Be careful," said Gyro. "Remember, I haven't tested it yet."

"It can't hurt," Donald declared. "My plants are so puny, I have nothing to lose."

Donald and Gyro ran back to Donald's house, and Donald pointed the spray gun at his little rose bush. "Now!" said Donald in a stern voice, and he began to spray.

For a second, nothing happened. Then the rose bush seemed to tremble and quiver, and suddenly there was a fresh green sprout on the bush—and another and another. Then there was a bud—and another and another. They grew and swelled and burst open, and

Donald and Gyro were staring at beautiful red roses.

"Gyro, it's terrific!" exclaimed Donald.

"It's so terrific, even I can't believe it," said Gyro, "and I invented it!"

"You'll make a fortune!" cried Donald. "And I'll have the biggest, best garden in town!"

Donald began to run to and fro, spraying everything he saw. He sprayed the pansies and the petunias and the morning glories. He sprayed the honeysuckle and the snapdragons.

"Wait till Daisy sees this!" he cried.

"She won't brag so much about her garden!"

Donald dropped the spray gun and ran into the house. He picked up the telephone to call Daisy.

Suddenly, "Yeow!" shouted Gyro. "Help!"

Donald dropped the telephone and spun around to see Gyro race in the door. Close behind Gyro came a giant tendril of a morning glory.

"Call the fire department!" yelled Gyro. "Quick!"

There was a crash, and a branch of the great rose bush burst in through the window and knocked over a lamp. Great masses of honeysuckle tumbled through another window, curled around the telephone, and yanked it right out of the wall.

"Run for it!" Gyro shouted.

Donald squawked and ran. He and Gyro raced out the back door just ahead of the morning glory. They clambered over the back fence with giant snapdragons snapping at their heels.

The moment he was safely outside the yard, Gyro sped to his workshop and snatched up a second spray gun. He shook and he trembled, but he managed to fill the spray gun with a formula he had invented the week before —a formula that made things small.

"I wondered how I would use this,"

said Gyro to himself. "Now I know."

Gyro dashed back to Donald's house. Donald was standing outside the fence, gaping at the rampaging roses and the madly climbing vines and the huge snapdragons and the giant petunias.

"I'll never get in my house again!" sobbed Donald.

"Yes, you will," promised Gyro. He began to spray, and he sprayed and sprayed and sprayed.

The monstrous snapdragons withered and shrank. The honeysuckle and the morning glories retreated. The petunias drooped. The rose was once again only a dry little bush without a single flower.

"Thank goodness!" said Donald. "Let's not try *that* again!"

"Don't worry," said Gyro, and he went right home and buried the formula for Speedy-Gro. He buried the formula that made things small, too. "Things are the size they are because that's the size they're supposed to be," said Gyro. "And I'm not going to tamper with them."

He didn't either. And from that day on, Donald watered his plants and fed them, the way most gardeners do. Some of the plants grew and bloomed. Some didn't. But that's the way it is with plants, and Donald didn't complain— except for just a little bit, now and then.

27

The McDuck Luck

Uncle Scrooge McDuck sobbed huge, sad sobs as he drove toward the top of Goblin Hill.

"My luck is failing me!" he moaned. "My new breakfast food factory is a flop! The breakfast food tastes . . . it tastes . . ."

"It tastes just awful!" said Huey Duck. He sat in the back seat and scowled at a box of something called Crunchie-Puffs.

"Anything that's made out of alfalfa stalks and dried seaweed is bound to taste awful," Dewey Duck pointed out.

"But Crunchie-Puffs are nourishing and also good for the teeth!" protested Uncle Scrooge.

"Who cares, if no one will eat them?" said Louie Duck.

"I made a dreadful mistake," said Uncle Scrooge. But then the old zillionaire brightened up. "Maybe one mistake

"Hey! It's nice here!" cried Dewey.

"And it's all mine!" said Uncle Scrooge. "Of course it's a shame that the trees will have to be cut down and the stream dammed up, but . . ."

"Unca Scrooge!" Huey exclaimed. "You're going to cut down the trees?"

"Why?" asked Louie.

"Because I'm going to build a second money bin here," said Scrooge.

"But the trees are beautiful!" said Dewey.

Scrooge nodded. "True. But what could be more beautiful than a money bin? And I got the land for practically nothing. Tomorrow I'll call the lumbermen and . . ."

"You'll call who?" said a deep, rumbly, grumbly voice behind Uncle Scrooge.

"Eh?" Uncle Scrooge looked around.

"Here I am, beside the thorn bush," said the grumbly, rumbly voice.

"My stars!" exclaimed Uncle Scrooge, for he was looking at a little man who was only waist-high to a duck. The little man had red hair and a red beard and a pair of bushy red eyebrows. He also had eyes like hard little black buttons, and he glared at Uncle Scrooge.

"Who are you, that you want to clear off our oak trees?" demanded the little man.

in a lifetime isn't too terrible," he decided. "Sooner or later I'll think of something to do with the Crunchie-Puffs. In the meantime, we can look over my new property on Goblin Hill. There's no way that can turn out to be a mistake!"

They were almost at the top of Goblin Hill when the road ended. Uncle Scrooge parked the car and he and the boys got out. They stood beneath giant oak trees. Robins and bluebirds flew overhead, calling to one another. They could hear baby birds chirping in their nests. They could see a stream of water that sparkled and bubbled as it ran over a bed of shining, smooth stones.

"I'm Scrooge McDuck and I own this land," announced Uncle Scrooge.

There was more mumbling and muttering and grumbling, and dozens of small creatures like the little one with the red beard came out from behind trees and bushes.

"Go away!" said one.

"Leave us in peace!" said another.

"Unca Scrooge," whispered Louie. "I have a feeling we shouldn't be here."

"Even if you do own the land," said Huey, in a timid voice, "I think we had better leave."

"Don't be silly," said Uncle Scrooge. He turned to the little fellow with the beard. "Now, my good man . . ." he began.

"Man?" said the small one. "What makes you think I'm a man? I'm a goblin, that's what I am. My name's Grunder." The little creature nodded toward his companions. "We're all goblins."

Dewey gasped. "So that's why they call it Goblin Hill!"

Uncle Scrooge looked somewhat distressed. But then he pulled himself up to his full height. "I'm sorry, but you're trespassing on my property," he announced. "This is a perfect spot for my second money bin, and this is where I intend to build it. You'll have to move."

"Money bin, eh?" said the red-bearded goblin. "That would be a place to keep money?"

"It would," said Uncle Scrooge.

"You've a lot of money?" asked the goblin.

"I'm the richest duck in the world," said Uncle Scrooge proudly.

"Build your money bin here, and we'll tunnel into it and carry off your gold," threatened old Grunder.

"You can't scare me," sneered Uncle Scrooge. "My money bin will be burglar proof."

"Ah, but we're not burglars," pointed out Grunder, in a rather reasonable way. "We're goblins, and we can get in where we please."

"Unca Scrooge, I bet they can," said Louie.

"Let's go!" urged Dewey.

"But I bought the land!" wailed Uncle Scrooge. "If I can't use it . . ."

"Then you made a mistake," said Huey.

"Two in one day," Scrooge shivered, and opened the car door. "My luck *is* changing," groaned Scrooge. "If things go on this way, soon I'll be a very poor old duck indeed."

Uncle Scrooge was so upset that he didn't seem to know what he was doing. He reached into the back seat of the car and took out a package of his dreadful new breakfast food. And he began to eat Crunchie-Puffs in a mournful, absent-minded way.

He didn't taste the seaweed. He didn't taste the alfalfa stalks, either. He was too distressed to really taste much of anything.

Old Grunder pointed to the box of Crunchie-Puffs in Uncle Scrooge's hand. "What's that?" he asked.

"Breakfast food," said Huey.

"You wouldn't like it," said Dewey.

"Nobody likes Crunchie-Puffs," said Louie. "But you can try them if you want to."

And Louie handed the box to the goblin.

The goblin nibbled a Crunchie-Puff and said, "Hmm!"

He nibbled a second one slowly and said, "Ahhh!"

He took a third one and cried, "Lovely!" Then he gulped down a whole handful.

The other goblins crowded around. "Have you more?" said one to Uncle Scrooge.

Uncle Scrooge did have several more boxes of Crunchie-Puffs in the car. In fact, he had lots. He gladly handed them to the goblins. In a twinkling the goblins had eaten all the Crunchie-Puffs— one, two, three!

Uncle Scrooge began to smile. "It so happens," said he to the goblins, "that I own the factory that makes these delicious, yummy treats. Now we might make a deal."

"Not if it means losing our trees," said the goblin Grunder.

"Then there's no deal!" cried Uncle Scrooge.

"Not so fast," said the goblin. "There are things in the world besides money bins." The goblin moved closer to Scrooge. "What do you think of diamonds?" he asked softly.

"Diamonds?" Scrooge blinked, "I think highly of diamonds."

"I've heard that mortals do," said the goblin. "Well, we've been digging diamonds out of the earth for centuries. We have more diamonds than most mortals see in a lifetime. We'll pay you a pound of diamonds for every pound of these . . . these . . ."

"Crunchie-Puffs!" cried Scrooge.

"Yes. A pound of diamonds for every pound of Crunchie-Puffs you deliver to our hill. But you're not to touch our trees and you're not to let anyone know we're here."

"I wouldn't dream of telling anyone you're here," said Uncle Scrooge. "And my nephews will be more than willing to hike up here twice a week to deliver the Crunchie-Puffs—and to bring back the diamonds."

So it was arranged. Huey, Dewey, and Louie *were* happy to hike up Goblin Hill twice a week and wander about under the trees and even fish in the cool, sparkling stream.

The goblins were happy, too. They seemed to like Crunchie-Puffs better than diamonds.

Uncle Scrooge was happiest of all. He hadn't made two mistakes in one day. He hadn't even made one mistake. "With the McDuck luck, all my mistakes turn into good deals," said Uncle Scrooge, "so I can keep on being the richest duck in the world."

And, since there was no danger that he would ever run out of Crunchie-Puffs, or that the goblins would ever run out of diamonds, that was exactly what happened.

Bug Off!

"I can't stand it!" said Donald Duck on the telephone. "Cousin Fethry's come to visit, and he's on a nature kick. He wants me to water my garden with rainwater instead of city water, because rainwater is nature's way."

"But it hasn't rained for weeks!" said Daisy.

"Try telling that to Fethry," said Donald. "You don't happen to have any rainwater around the house, do you?"

"I'm afraid not," laughed Daisy. "And I'm glad that Fethry's your cousin and not mine."

Daisy hung up then, and went out to sit under the big beech tree in her backyard and read her book. She had not read long before she heard someone say, "Sad! Very sad!"

Daisy looked up and blinked. Then she almost said, "Drat!" Or possibly, "Blast!" For Donald's cousin Fethry was looking over the fence, examining her tree.

"I don't have any rainwater," said Daisy quickly.

"No one does," said Fethry. "That's one of the things that is sad."

Fethry climbed the fence and came to stand under the tree. "Tragic!" he said, shaking his head. "Aphids! Do you know you have aphids in your beautiful tree!"

"I'll get the bug spray," said Daisy.

"Bug spray?" Fethry cried.

"Of course," said Daisy. "If I have aphids in my tree, I'd better get rid of them, hadn't I?"

"But not with nasty old bug spray!" protested Fethry. "You'll get rid of them in nature's own way."

"I will?" said Daisy.

"Leave it to me," said Fethry, and he ran off.

He was back very soon with a box that had little airholes in it. "Ladybird beetles," he explained. "They eat aphids. I collected a bunch of them, in case I should meet anyone who's much troubled with aphids."

"I wasn't much troubled before you came along," said Daisy.

Fethry wasn't listening. He was opening his box. And he truly had collected hundreds of ladybugs. They swarmed out of the box and flew here and there. They settled on Daisy's tree and her hedges and her flowers and grass, and a number of them settled on Daisy herself.

"Fethry, there's got to be an easier way!" cried Daisy.

"Now, now, now!" said Fethry. "Mustn't upset yourself. Ladybugs are innocent, harmless little creatures. I'll just run and get a whisk broom and brush you off."

And Fethry dashed into the house.

"Fethry!" screamed Daisy. "Shut the screen door!"

Too late. It seemed to Daisy that at least a zillion ladybugs flew into her kitchen.

Daisy did say, "Blast!" She also said, "Drat!" several times. She picked up her book, as if she wanted to swat someone with it. Then she reminded herself that Fethry was a guest, after

all, even if she hadn't actually invited him, and she went into the house.

Fethry was rummaging in the broom closet, looking for a whisk broom. There were ladybugs on the counters and ladybugs on the stove and ladybugs on the refrigerator.

"The bug spray is under the sink," said Daisy.

"Daisy, you couldn't!" shrieked Fethry. "You couldn't spray these kind, beneficial little beetles, intended by nature to . . ."

"To eat aphids," said Daisy. "But there aren't any aphids in my house!"

"Well then," said Fethry, "you really don't need the ladybugs in here."

"I do not!" said Daisy "I don't need them! I don't want them! I didn't ask for them, and . . ."

"Why didn't you say so?" asked Fethry, looking at her.

"Aaaagh!" screamed Daisy.

"Such a temper!" said Fethry. He seized an empty jar that was standing on a counter, punched several holes in the lid, then began to pick up the ladybugs. He did it carefully, one bug at a time.

"That's going to take you quite a while," said Daisy.

"I'm afraid so," Fethry answered.

"Well, you keep at it," said Daisy. "I have an errand to do."

And Daisy brushed several ladybugs off her dress and went out. She got into her car and drove away.

It was almost dark when Daisy came home again. She looked dusty and mussy, and even a bit muddy, but she also looked quite pleased. She had a nice big box which had airholes in it.

"I got all the ladybugs," said Fethry. "Except the ones in the backyard. I'll leave them, in case you're troubled with aphids again."

"Thank you very much, Fethry," said Daisy.

"It was nothing," said Fethry.

"But it was," said Daisy. "It certainly was something. I'll never forget it. And to show my appreciation, I have a gift for you."

"Oh?" said Fethry.

"In case you're troubled with flies," said Daisy.

"Odd that you should think of that," said Fethry. "There were a few flies buzzing around Donald's guest room when I left there today."

"How nice," said Daisy. "This will take care of them in nature's own way." She handed the box to Fethry. "Make sure you don't open it until you're back in Donald's guest room, with the door closed."

"You're too kind," said Fethry.

"Not always," said Daisy, and she watched Fethry go off with his jar of ladybugs under one arm and the box that she had given him tucked snugly under the other.

Before long, the telephone rang. It was Donald calling.

"How did you manage that?" Donald asked. "Fethry's up in his room screaming that the place is full of frogs. And it is."

"Nature's way of getting rid of houseflies," said Daisy smugly.

"It may be nature's way of getting rid of house guests," said Donald. "Fethry's packing to leave."

"Tell him to take his ladybugs with him," Daisy ordered.

Fethry did take the ladybugs. He also took his battered old suitcase, and he took the train out of town.

And Donald took Daisy to the movies that night. "I'm keeping the guest-room door shut and leaving the frogs where they are," he reported, as they drove downtown.

"I'm glad," said Daisy. "They're fine frogs. It took me hours to catch them all."

"Right," said Donald. "So it'll be good to have them on hand, in case Fethry decides to come back."

Which he didn't.

Not for a long, long time.

Which suited Daisy Duck to a tee.

Go Slow, Stop Often

"I wish Goofy would get back with the boys," said Mickey Mouse to Minnie. "We'll be late for the movie if they don't hurry."

Mickey Mouse and Minnie, and Daisy Duck and Donald were out in front of Goofy's house, looking anxiously up the street.

"Where did Goofy take the kids today?" asked Daisy.

"To a picnic at Morgan's Meadow," said Mickey. "They were going on the old river road."

"Don't worry," said Minnie. "They'll be all right."

"Oh, I know they'll be all right. Goofy can't drive too fast in that old car of his, and there's never any traffic on the river road. They're safe enough, but they're always so late."

Mickey heard a clattering, chugging sound from down the street, and Goofy's broken-down, wobbly old car rattled around the corner.

"Hi, Uncle Mickey!" called Morty Mouse.

"Boy, did we have fun!" said Ferdie.

The car pulled up and stopped and Huey Duck leaped out. "Look, Unca Donald! I caught two frogs in the swamp," he reported.

"Can we put them in Unca Scrooge's bed and make him yell?" asked Louie Duck.

"Frogs?" said Mickey. "Swamp? What swamp?"

"The one where we stopped to change the flat tire," explained Louie Duck.

"No wonder you're late," said Mickey Mouse.

"Shucks, Mick," drawled Goofy, "it

43

wasn't the flat tire held us up so much. It was the rear bumper. Darn thing kept falling off the car. We stopped three times to pick it up."

Daisy Duck's nieces, April, May, and June, hopped out of the back seat.

"I found a four-leaf clover when we stopped near Henderson's barn," said April.

"And I picked a bunch of violets when we stopped near Farber's woods," said May.

"That's why it took you all day and half the night," said Daisy Duck. And she started for home with the girls.

"You can't put those frogs in Uncle Scrooge's bed," Donald warned his nephews, and they went off.

Morty and Ferdie thanked Goofy for a keen day, and he grinned. "I had a better time than you did," he said "Want to go again next Saturday?"

"That'd be great!" said Morty.

Mickey smiled. "It *would* be great, Goofy," he said. "The kids have a wonderful time with you. But next Saturday, why don't you take my car? The bumpers hardly ever fall off, and maybe you'll get home before midnight."

"Aw, Mick, it isn't midnight yet," said Goofy.

"No, but it's almost dark," Mickey pointed out.

And so, the next Saturday, Donald's nephews and Daisy's nieces and Morty and Ferdie set out with Goofy. They had Mickey's car, which could go as fast as a car should go, and which didn't rattle or clank or pop or hiss or boil over. They weren't going on the old river road. They were going on the new express highway. And they weren't going to Morgan's Meadow, either. They were going all the way to Brewster's Park, fifty miles from home.

And they were back on time that day. Indeed, it was only midafternoon when Goofy and the carload of kids came down the street and stopped in front of Mickey's house.

"Have a nice time?" asked Mickey.

"Yep," said Goofy, but he didn't seem too sure about it.

"Did you catch any frogs?" Mickey asked Huey, Dewey, and Louie Duck.

"How could we?" said Huey.

"There weren't any frogs at Brewster's Park," said Dewey.

"And this car doesn't break down anyplace where there *are* frogs. It doesn't break down anyplace at all," said Louie.

"Did you find any four-leaf clovers?" Mickey asked April, May, and June.

"How could we?" asked April.

"There weren't any at Brewster's Park," said May.

"And the bumper didn't fall off on the way home, so we couldn't hunt for four-leaf clovers," said June.

"Did you have fun?" Mickey asked his nephews.

"Oh, sure, sure!" said Morty.

"It was . . . it was just like we planned it," said Ferdie. But he said it as if that wasn't quite the best way for plans to work.

The kids took their picnic baskets and straggled away, and Goofy shook his head. "I think we made a mistake,

Mick," he said nodding his head slowly.

"I think so," agreed Mickey Mouse.

"I know that next week will be different," said Goofy.

"Right," said Mickey.

The next week *was* different. The kids were at Goofy's house at dawn, and they piled into Goofy's goofy old car, with the bumpers that kept falling off and the tires that so often went flat and the engine that chugged. And they set out along the old river road for Morgan's Meadow.

They got back late. Of course they got back late. The streetlights were already burning, but no one scolded.

How could anyone scold Goofy? His radiator had boiled over three times on the trip, and the rear bumper had fallen off twice, and one tire had gone flat once.

But April had seen a tree all covered with butterflies.

May had picked a pretty flower.

Morty had caught some pollywogs in the swamp. He had carried them home in a jar so that he could keep them and watch them grow into frogs.

Huey Duck had caught a praying mantis, and he had it in a box. He was going to take it home so that it would eat up all the bugs in Donald's garden.

"Have a good time?" asked Mickey, when the kids had gone chattering off.

"Best ever," said Goofy happily. "Half the fun is in getting there and getting back. Just so you remember to go slow and stop often—and with my clunky old car, who could forget?"